TYRANNOSAURUS
(tye-ran-o-**sawr**′-us)

ALLOSAURUS
(al-lo-**sawr**′-us)

CAMPTOSAURUS
(kamp-to-**sawr**′-us)

STEGOSAURUS
(steg-o-**sawr**′-us)

DIMETRODON
(dye-**met**′-ro-don)

PROCOMPSOGNATHUS
(pro-comp-so-**nath**′-us)

For my parents

300 million years ago many amphibians lived along the swampy shores of the earth. Eryops lived on the land but returned to the water to lay eggs.

Eryops
5 feet long

DINOSAURS!

Illustrations and text by Anthony Rao

Platt & Munk, Publishers/New York
A Division of Grosset & Dunlap

Dimetrodon
10 feet long

Edaphosaurus
7 feet long

Dimetrodon and Edaphosaurus were reptiles, or lizards, that lived 50,000 years before the true dinosaurs roamed the earth. The smaller of the two, Edaphosaurus, ate plants, while the larger Dimetrodon ate Edaphosaurus—or any other raw meat.

Procompsognathus
2 feet long

Plant-eating Plateosaurus was one of the first dinosaurs. Like most dinosaurs, Plateosaurus laid eggs. Small meat-eating dinosaurs, like little Procompsognathus, sometimes stole these eggs for food.

Plateosaurus
21 feet long

**Brontosaurus
70 feet long**

One of the largest dinosaurs ever to walk the earth
was a plant-eater named Brontosaurus. Brontosaurus
was as long as five automobiles and weighed 30 tons.
Scientists think that it probably had to spend most of its
time in the water, which helped carry its weight.

Allosaurus
30 feet long

Camptosaurus
4 to 15 feet long

Compsognathus
1 foot long

Allosaurus may have been a fierce meat-eater, but it had a brain about the size of a walnut. Its powerful legs helped it when chasing its meals—often the gentle plant-eating Camptosaurus. The tiny Compsognathus was the smallest known dinosaur. It was only as big as a chicken.

Stegosaurus was a plant-eater that weighed four tons. The stiff plates on its back and the sharp spikes on its tail must have made Stegosaurus less than tempting to its meat-eating cousins.

Brachiosaurus was the tallest of the dinosaurs—often forty feet high. It had nostrils on the top of its head so that it was able to submerge its entire body in the water, except for the very tip of its head, through which it was able to breathe.

Brachiosaurus
80 feet long

Stegosaurus
25 feet long

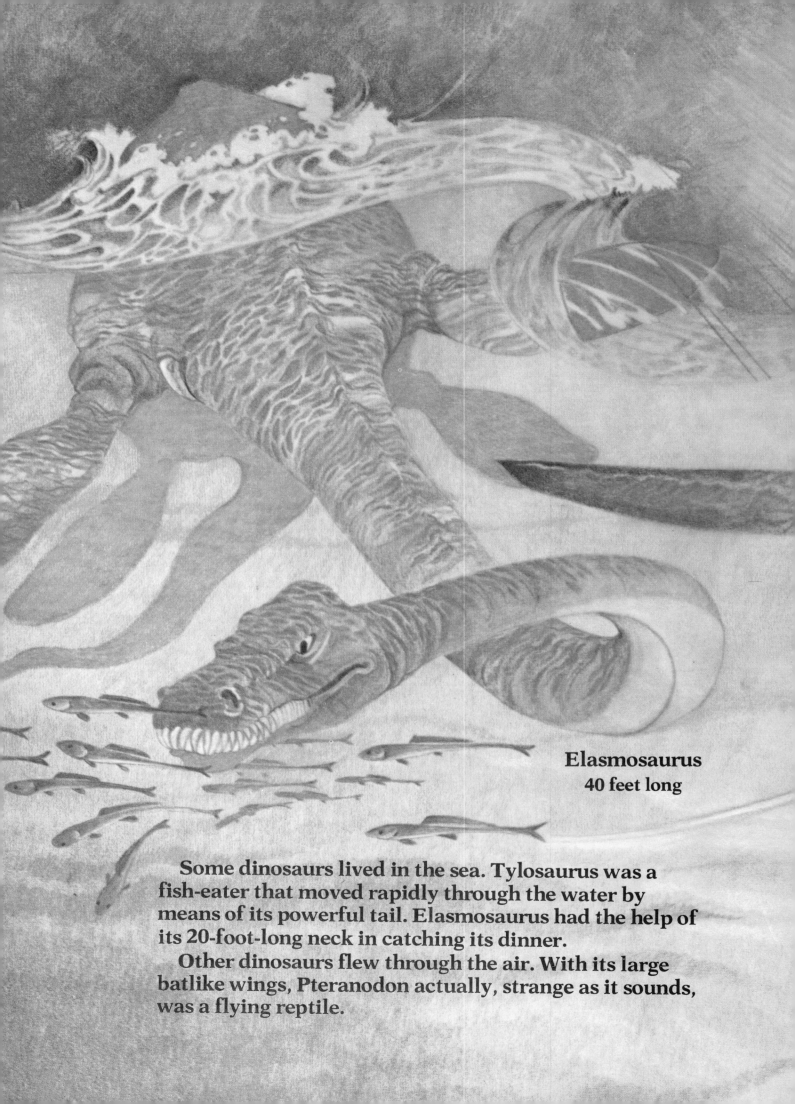

Elasmosaurus
40 feet long

Some dinosaurs lived in the sea. Tylosaurus was a fish-eater that moved rapidly through the water by means of its powerful tail. Elasmosaurus had the help of its 20-foot-long neck in catching its dinner.

Other dinosaurs flew through the air. With its large batlike wings, Pteranodon actually, strange as it sounds, was a flying reptile.

Pteranodon
7 foot wingspread

Tylosaurus
25 feet long

Parasaurolophus
40 feet long

Ornithomimus
14 feet long

Parasaurolophus had a strange, crest-shaped head. Scientists think that perhaps the crest held extra air so that Parasaurolophus could breathe under water.

Ornithomimus was a dinosaur that looked much like an ostrich of today.

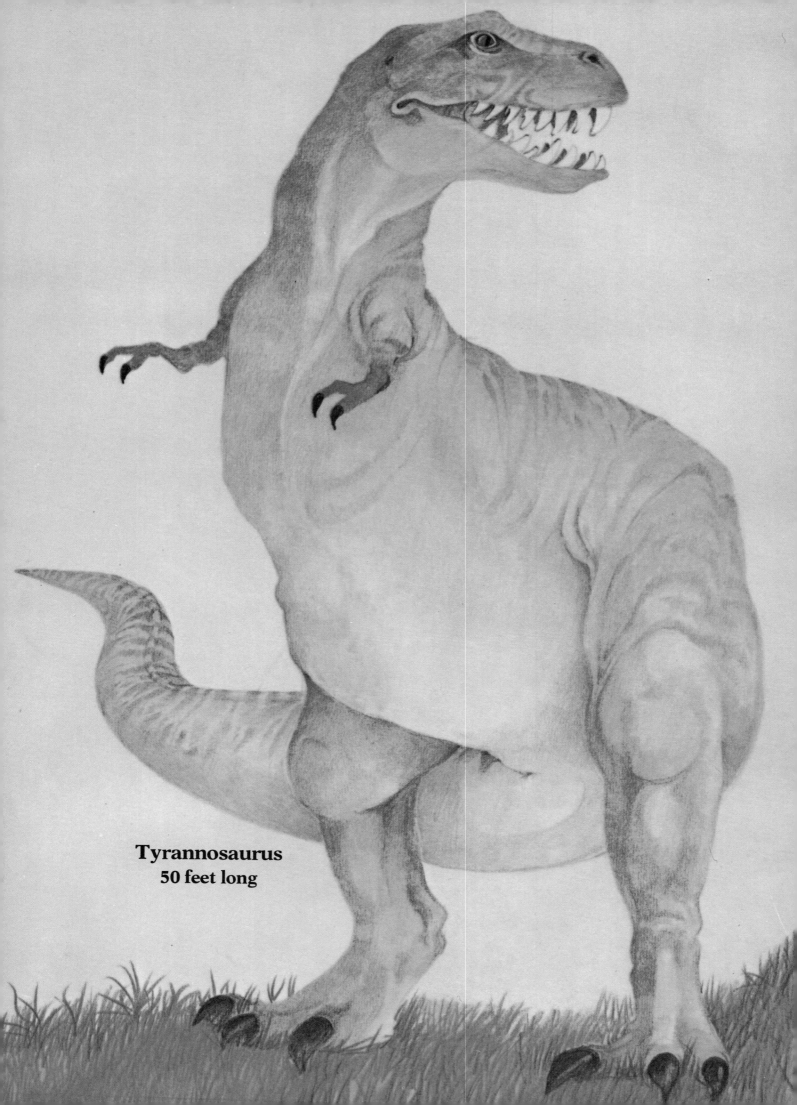

Tyrannosaurus
50 feet long

Triceratops
30 feet long

Tyrannosaurus was the largest and fiercest of all meat-eating dinosaurs. It stood taller than a two-story house and, with its great jaws and six-inch teeth, must have been the terror of its time.

One of the few plant-eaters that stood a chance against Tyrannosaurus was the three-horned Tryceratops. The armorlike plate at the back of its head protected it from just such an enemy as Tyrannosaurus.

Today there are no more dinosaurs.
But if you take a close look around you,
you'll notice something very
interesting . . .